WOMAN OF THE WIND

Mike
meeting you is
feeling the delicat
tenderness within
you has been
a blessing
Love Momfeather

The Wisdom of Momfeather
Book One

Published by SpiritWords, Inc.

For information, contact SpiritWords, Inc., 42 Walden Way,
Eliot, Maine 03903. *www.spiritwords.com*

SpiritWords, Inc.
ISBN 0-9711086-6-8

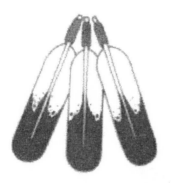

A special thanks to my husband
Dean who has so lovingly
supported my efforts.

The artwork was done by
Laura Hill, Canyon, Texas
Dwight O. Crowe, Cherokee, North Carolina
Used by permission.

WOMAN OF THE WIND

Woman of the wind sits alone atop Creation,

letting the wind blow her falling tresses.

Leaving open all the doors to feel the

vibration....feeling grounded in ancient

spiritual tradition and listening to the music

of this quiet intimate world. Sound is a

wonderful part of her, it is a stairway to a

higher consciousness. Thoughts and prayers

should be spent with confidence. It gives a

greater bond with the Creator. The Creator

is ever present in her world as she feels the

need to accept and give creatively. She

opens the door to her heart and allows

phenomenal things to happen. She embraces

the wind and realizes that she is a creative

being working with and within a greater whole.

A WOMAN OF THE WIND

A Little Girl's Dream

The morning was warm and sunny as I stood by the roadside. I pulled off the road where the driveway was some 50 years ago, to my Uncle Still's house. The memories flooded my mind as I walked through the two posts that once held the gate I would swing on as a child. I walked around the stones that held the cabin once filled with laughter. I could smell the cornbread and fried apples. The bacon was frying and the coffee perking on an open hearth. It was so good to be home and listen to the stories of yesterday echo in my mind. A magical smile crossed my face as I headed toward the old barn and down the trail to the creek. The old rose bush was still at the edge of the creek. I sat on that same big boulder and watched the petals fall softly into the water and float away. I floated with the petals many times and went to far away places. I would fantasize the stops along the way and my mind relived them today like yesterday. Some things do remain the same 50 years later…A LITTLE GIRL'S DREAMS

Dance of Love

Dancing in the sunshine of
my life, the dance of love,
as it leaps to the outer
realms of my heart. I am in
amazement at the feelings
that have carved their lines
deep into the passages of my
inner world. It is like a
new Springtime and the
growth has begun with the
gentle wind and the tiny
droplets of rain that cover
everything with a tiny shimmering
veil. These feelings of oneness
add new vision and splendor to
my life. Time has now locked
this dance of love.

8

A Warrior's Spirit Sings

Deep into the night beneath the
dark cloudless sky, the old warrior sat waiting
to walk in spiritual beauty.
He looked at the stars and felt the many spirits
gone before. He rejoiced in the realization
that he too would soon join them.
He knew his passing would bring
good things to follow.
He looked at the moon and
glimpsed the spirits of the birds.
He smiled at the spirit of the deer and
listened to the night birds as they spoke.
He had lived a good long life, and now accepts
his timeless journey. The strength and
love for his people had been his fortress.
It was time for eternal rest.
He smiled at the heavens
and sang his spirit to the sky,
deep in the night.

Spiritual Care

We sometimes lose track of our own spirit.
We reach for material things
or search among friends for comfort.
In the end peace, joy and happiness, all that
we search for, will come from within.
Our body is only an instrument that houses the spirit.
The spirit is what we need to feed and understand.
When I am taking care of the spirit I feel good
about myself. I like to call these special times,
loose threads that I haven't woven yet. I feel divine
protection and reach out with confidence for the quiet
peace that sings in silence just inside the garden of
serenity. I leave my footprints in the garden
and return to my world with joy and happiness.
I enjoy the quiet beauty of my surroundings and wish
to open my heart and soul for the gentle magic.

Daughter of Creation

I am born of Mother Earth; I have felt
the calling of the Creator from within. I feel blessed
and filled with love and joy. I allow this flow to
happen. I leave myself open for creation. Moving in
the direction of my dreams allows me to move closer
to my divinity. Mother Earth is my home. I feel safe
and protected with her at all times. I accept guidance
from within, from people and from situations. I treat
myself gently and allow myself to be vulnerable.

I accept myself today as I am, without need for
perfection. I honor the wisdom of life. I learn from all
I encounter. I extend my heart and hand. I reach for
my wisdom and my compassion to aid others. Lasting
friendships seem to find me. I am a lover of life, even
in times of sorrow and anxiety. I comfort myself by
comforting the world, by cherishing life; I allow life to
cherish me. I am able to love without demands. My
love is fluid, flexible, committed and it allows people
and events to unfold as needed. My heart explores the
world with wonder. My life advances through my
attitudes and actions. I am an Indian Woman.

I feel as one with the Earth Mother.

I am a Daughter of Creation.

Aho. Momfeather

Easily Amused

I am easily amused by the most simple things --
at dawn's light the streaming sun rays pour
through the leaves of the old oak tree in the back yard.
The daisies still drenched with dew, look like
lumps of gold as they shimmer in the morning sun.
I sit here to watch the morning come to life.
It does not take long for the show to start
as the raccoon creeps out from the bush
to eat corn that has been dropped from the birdfeeders.
The excitement is heightened when the acrobatic
oriole balances upside down on a twig to sneak a drink
from the hummingbirds' feeder. I watch all of this
to the music of the birds and insects that love to sing
the praises of the early dawn. Nearby the robin
splashes lavishly in the bird bath, flinging water with
the excitement of a child. A beautiful butterfly flies in
to share my glass of orange juice.
What a wonderful morning.
<u>I do wish you were here.</u>

Trust in Yourself

Trust in yourself—be your own best friend.
I do believe in myself and those around me.
I believe in creativity. Being creative goes beyond
the artist, the poet, or doing a craft.
Decide you can do something and do it.
Associate yourself with others who believe in
themselves and you. See yourself as being beautiful
and unique. When you go creative others notice
and the positive from you adds positive to those
in your presence. Set aflame your creative desires and
follow your dreams. Trust in yourself and
be your own best friend.

A Little Child

A little child filled with innocence and love
sits at my feet waiting to be fed the wonders of life.
I look at the sparkling eyes and the smile on the face
as I start to weave the web of life.
The things I say will last forever if given with love.
Cherish your freedom my child, act, think, feel,
and choose wisely. Accept the responsibility
that comes with your choices. The choices you make
will shape your life. Set forth on a gentle path and
know you have the power to change the world.
Refuse negative thoughts and pick up the positive.
I believe in you. Remember always the world is work
in progress and you can make a difference.

Fragrant Breezes

While visiting a friend, I take a book to the
center of her flower garden for some quiet time.
I find a chair and sit back, close my eyes.
First the spicy fragrance of the trees and
the floral enchantment combined with the rapture
of honeysuckle tickle my senses as they are swept
across the garden by a friendly breeze.
Keeping my eyes closed, I can imagine
tiny pink roses on satin banners floating gently
across the garden, sharing their delicate fragrance
with everyone. I smell the faintest odor of violets.
My mind goes to the tiny purple symbols of romance
and summers wooing. Other exotic scents
ride the wind and tickle my senses.

Thunder Beings

The thunder-beings march to the sound
of many drums. I listen to many soft drum
rolls as they march in perfect order
across the northern sky and over the prairie.
As they move across the sky, they are joined
by the brightness of the lightening. Their
drums become louder and as the lightening
comes you can feel the vibrations of the
thunder-beings and wait breathlessly for the next
light, hoping to see the thunder as it marches away.
You can sense the moisture in the air. You hear, see,
and feel the power of your natural surroundings. I sit
waiting for a touch of magic and suddenly the ancient
waters touch down all around me. I feel blessed
to share this natural phenomenon
in a special way. Thanks for sharing a
magic moment.

Silence

The sound of silence comes from within.
It allows you to hear the impossible, if you listen for
the sounds of silence. The sound of the snowflakes as
they fall in lacy elegance from the heavens.
They do a special dance in rhythm as they touch down
on Mother Earth. The sounds of the stars that twinkle
in the night—listen, you can hear them moving
delicately out in space, sliding and gliding each taking
its place. The silent growth sounds of the trees as you
sit in quietude listening to its life sounds. The bark
cracks and the leaves thunder as you ponder its beauty.
The melodious sounds of the wind as it glides with the
greatest of ease through my hair as it travels to the
pasture and beyond. The quiet silence of a tender
raindrop as it falls into place. It splashes across
my face and I hear trickling sounds as it runs away.
The magical sounds you hear from within seem to
demand their own galaxy. Your heart beats, your blood
rushes in silent splendor through your veins.
I love the quiet delicate sounds of silence I hear
when I close my eyes and hear the memories
tiptoe across my mind in silence.

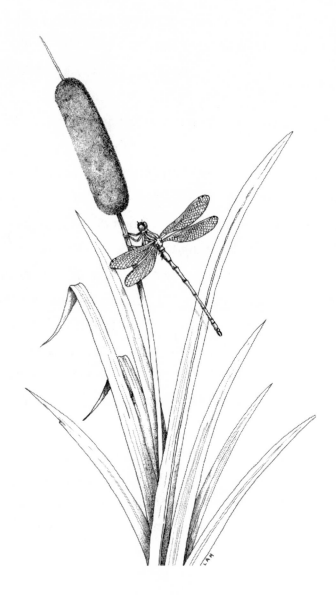

Near Valley Forge

Pennsylvania Countryside, near Valley Forge.
I stopped by a rolling hill, it is a delectable morning,
sun shining, warm breezes and the view is spectacular.
I cannot help but wonder how this place looked two
hundred and fifty years ago, before the battle. The
dance of the sunbeams has cast their shadows on a
nostalgic covered bridge. It has been painted white and
the brightness adds a special touch to the lush green
carpet of grass. I can't help but notice the calmness of
the clouds and the soft gentle flow of the water, as the
beautiful horses graze idly in the foreground. The tiny
bush beside me is covered with buds and much to my
delight a beautiful dragonfly with its aqua blue body
and black lacey wings stops on a leaf to say good
morning and disappears. The deer appears out of
nowhere, under the tree to check out the area. The
brightness of the early morning sun leaves a white
etching around it. She decides that all is well and
starts to graze without fear. What a glorious morning.
I am blessed with such beautiful surroundings.

Your Treasure Chest

At times I wonder why people become
so enchanted with others that they do
not see their own treasure chest. I want my treasures
to shine. Each friend I have is an added gemstone,
each day is a new sparkle. I allow myself to become
like a tidal wave, so my life can empty and fill
according to need. When I suffer I know that a new
gift will come. I choose to accept that which comes
and give thanks. The seasons of our life have
meaning. While looking into your treasure chest throw
away the dull and tarnished items. They will take away
the beauty of all your shining gems. Give new
reason to the seasons in your life.

Seaside Morning

Trying this morning to choose, which
to watch. The naked sea or
the cloudless sky. I will wait in silence
as the sky dresses itself in soft pink
billowing clouds, edged with light
blue lace in the early dawn or I could
watch the naked sea do its
shimmering dance as it gently touches
the morning sky. It is seemingly an
endless dance as I watch this
seaside morning come to
life and the choice was made for
me as I watch two birds off
in the distant horizon decorate
an already beautiful sky. The
morning passes swiftly, now,
seemingly white walls of clouds
drift in like white shadowing overlay
on the once pink clouds. The shadows
seem to dance on the naked sea.
Both the sea and the sky seem to be
convulsing in the same breath.
A work of art and wonder
in my beautiful world.

With Your Eyes Closed

Last evening, alone in the stillness of the
quiet deep wilderness, I sat and closed
my eyes. I felt the presence of life
without seeing it. I could feel the
energy of the sweet smelling earth and
knew of her great mysteries. I knew
the huge rock that I was leaning on
held ancient wisdom. The trees
sing songs to me and I listen. The
animals talk and I know their voices
and hear their thoughts. All the birds
fall in perfect harmony with the
wind as it blows across the placid
waters of the shallow pool that lies
in the center of this dense wooded area.
These are the tiny miracles I see with my eyes closed.

YOUR LOVE

Prayer and blessings are present
daily in my life. I listen
to hear the life sounds. Acute
senses help determine my
direction. My heart presents
a courtyard-like setting with
a fountain that forever flows
with my love. I no longer
fear my abilities as I touch the
lives of others. The powerful
feelings are now understood as
I take your hand this day,
I walk into another reality,
into another world of perception.
There is a delicate beauty on this path.
A gift that you offered and I accepted.
YOUR LOVE

Butterflies

Everyday I am amazed by the magic of the seasons. Everything from smelling the strange exotic scent of the mimosa as it comes in with the south wind to the gurgling streams. Magic is seeing the butterfly and watching the cycle from egg clusters, to little brown caterpillars with yellow bands, to the chrysalis. The daily changes always amaze me. What would a summer stroll be without the butterflies? They are everywhere, over the meadows, in the backyard and over the hills. Every flower is touched with the beauty and grace of the butterfly. I am always in awe of the vibrant hues as they flutter from place to place across the dew-drenched and lovely gardens. A tiger swallowtail is basking on the cranberry flower and adds a splash of dazzling color as he soaks up the sun. Another beautiful black and yellow butterfly perches itself on a lantana bloom. I love the summer magic as I watch the butterflies.

They remind me of flying flowers!

Golden Threads

Golden threads of sun weave
themselves around me this bright early
morning. Spring is everywhere, the grass,
and the trees, even the birds know it is
spring as they sing the songs of new
life and sharing. The tiny beads of
moisture from the heavy dew seem to
bathe me. It is cool, refreshing and a
reminder of the magic it holds. I walk
a short distance and the sun is graciously
sharing its warmth as it smiles at me
over the hillside. I enjoy the gleaming
strands of light that seem to penetrate
my inner world. I can feel the wondrous
warmth as the golden threads weave
themselves around me. What a glorious
moment I have to share….

I Did It

What a beautiful day to be driving....
Catching glimpses of the birds as they gracefully
swoop across the sky.
The Sun is shining brightly and the barns seem to be a
brighter red and the lush vegetation greener.
The planted fields are picture perfect and the
blue of the sky magnificent.
The wind touches the tops of the tall grass;
it sways with the wind, bows gracefully and returns to
its position. I want to feel the gentleness of the breeze
that moves these grasses. I want the grasses to touch
my skin. I want to feel the motion of the tiny seeds as
they move. Of course I need to stop the car,
get out and feel this natural Phenomenon.
Now ask me if I did it...???
YOU KNOW I DID!

Choices

I awoke this morning to the beautiful light of another
day and the songs of the winged ones. I thank the
Creator for all He has provided for all of us.
The choices I make will make a difference around me.
I stop long enough to think of how these choices
will affect others.
I do not know what is on either side of the path I walk,
but I do know that walking the center will help me
keep my balance. As the morning becomes lighter
and the shades of the night have passed,
I prepare myself to be a bridge today. One that will
help others cross to a more peaceful place.
I wish to share love and joy in the spirit,
mind and hearts of others today.
I have a choice.

Walk Toward Your Dreams

Walk toward your dreams.
Vibrations of life are meaningful and joyful.
The world is full of love and miracles.
I am enchanted by all; the wonder of the water;
the growth of the trees; the vibrations of the stones
and the faces of the people.
I see and feel the beauty of my surroundings,
and the harmony of my friendships.
I always take the time to appreciate the many
small gifts that have brought me delight and
renewed spirit. I hold tenderness in my heart
for my past and my present, realizing it is all a
part of me, creating and molding my future.
Simplify your life; live your life
as you have imagined and walk with confidence
toward your dreams.

Tiny Dandelion

The tiny dandelion sings with endurance.
It clings to Mother Earth in the early Spring.
It sings the songs of the spring wind,
looks up at the sun and gathers strength.
The dandelion begs for the Spring rain,
grows strong during the day and sleeps at night.
The flower encircles itself with scent,
and dreams of the warm summer wind
that will carry its seeds into flight.
The little dandelion knows that it is a great
part of a whole. I am enraptured with delight
as I watch the tiny dandelion sing.

The Mighty Oak

Stopping at a rest area somewhere in Illinois,
I walk down a path that leads me to a stream.
A beautiful oak tree seems to reach out to me.
Its energy calls to me but I keep walking
down the path toward the small stream of water.
I stop with delight on an old covered bridge
with dated and carved initials of loves gone by.
It is a place of romantic charm and splendor
of the past. I look over the edge of the bridge and
see a rock that I would love to have at the waters edge.
I start to retrieve it and notice that it seemed to be
doing sentry duty for a larger stone.
I did not wish to hinder the natural duty of the stone so
I left it. I walk away from the bridge and the water.
Again I feel the spirit of the beautiful oak tree calling
me. I walk to the tree give it a hug and feel the energy.
Walked away with a smile on my face and the wonder
of the ageless tree in my heart.
Aho

Listen and Respond

Today listen and respond to your own needs.
Trust yourself and follow your own light.
Listen carefully and have the courage to ask for help
when needed. Embrace your dark side as well as the
light side, for without both you will lose your balance.
See the universe in everyone. Feel the love and
passion of the universe within yourself. The most
thrilling and passionate thing in the universe is falling
in love with yourself. Life is unlimited and flowing
with energy. Be in touch with the purpose of your life.
Be truthful and honest with others. Our bodies express
our individual perfection. We are all our own person,
a force and light to be reckoned with. Today listen
and respond to your own needs.

The Circle

Everything must complete the Circle.
I watch the blossoms of Spring as they
arrive on the misty wind.
I watch their response to the tender misty rain.
I think of them as tiny Spring footprints
as they arrive in every color, shape and size.
Some on a short stem, others on the ground,
or bush, while others are in the tallest tree.
Many very durable, others fragile with strange
exotic scents, and others have saucy smiles.
They seem to boast their own touch of beauty,
none want to be like the other.
Beautiful, happy and content to take their walk
and return to Mother Earth without question.
From the smallest blossom to the towering oak
they embrace the world around them taking only
what they need to complete their Circle.
Such magical things happen in the natural world!

A Love Poem

It is an honor for me to have you in my life.
I have experienced the joy of true sharing
from my heart to yours. The way our spirits smile at
each other brings laughter to our soul.
When I am feeling fragile and broken,
you seal the seams and melt the jagged edges.
I know what it means to love without condition and to
be as one with another. When you came into my life
you gave me the sun strands by day and the moon
glow at night, helping me to create wholeness in my
life. I have indeed been bathed in luxury.
My darling, my husband, my life.
Thank you Creator.

Half Full?

If we change the way we think,
we can change the world around us.
We can live a richer, fuller life
if we open our eyes and accept
our natural world. We can create
a more bountiful existence.
This gives us the opportunity
to surrender to a deeper flow of life
and be able to cherish all we encounter.
I have been asked if my glass is half full
or half empty…my answer is I do not want
a half empty glass for I could never fill it,
but if it is half full, I am working
on filling it. I want it to overflow
with my own intellectual interest.
I am deeply touched by the diversity
of those I choose to share my life with
and fill my glass.

Late Spring

Leaving my shelter, I give thanks.
I know my morning has been blessed with
the crispness of late Spring.
I was enraptured with the stillness that seems
to come from all directions as I stand
before the Creator.
I thank Him for my day that has now begun.
I enjoy the presence of Mother Earth and
appreciate all she has given us. Looking upward
at Grandfather Sky I want to sense the joy
He must feel to be surrounding the Earth Mother.
He is holding no clouds this morning,
just embracing the new life which is in
abundance in late Spring.
Giving thanks for a beautiful day.
Aho

Blues

Today I collected the blues.
There are many ways to see the blues…
on the wings of a beautiful bird
on the top of the mountain,
looking down at the blue misty valley,
the crystal blue of the spring sky
or the deepest blue of the ocean.
I remember the blue hills among
the summer leaves and then a different
shade of blue in the winter.
I can see the exquisite shades of blue
as the sea washes against the white beaches.
The different shades of blue as you face
the many mountain ranges and the light
and fluffy blue white shades of snow.
The blue haze of the prairies and the
blue-purple hue of the tiny cornflower.

WOULD YOU LIKE A HANDFUL OF MY BLUES?

Sing the Songs

Sing the songs of the ancestors,
their drums still beat softly on the winds of time.
Listen to the wisdom of the Grandmothers.
Share their dreams with the young ones,
plant the seeds the Elders hid within us.
Seek the counsel of the Grandfathers,
they show us the pathway to ancient living.
Let your life be the door for the ancient ways to travel.
When we are tired their words will strengthen us.
When we are cold their love will warm us.
Listen with your heart and you will hear.

Home

Home where the wildflowers grow in radiant colors
and the killdeer trills can be heard at the road's edge.
Mother Earth's lush fragrance carpets the path
for my feet. I have returned to the peaceful quiet
I once called home. I have returned and found my
refuge. The seasons flow here in the mountains with
slow gentle fervor and I will again listen
to the low soft toned cadence of my family's speech
and laughter. I have arrived. I am home again
where I can watch the drowsy cattle graze
and write my thoughts, dream my dreams
to the pleasant rhythms of the
mountain streams.

Smiling

Smile softly for me today
as I will be smiling for you.
I want your spirit before me,
so I can feel the softness, listen to
the haunts and fears of the past.
I will reach out to you as the tears sting your cheeks.
You can run from the love that I give
and I will understand. I know the depth of your fears
and felt the depth of your love. I do not know
where you are going or where you have been.
I will always be your friend.
Smile softly for me today and
I will be smiling for you.

My Backyard

Having breakfast and beholding the beauty
outside my door. The robins sprinkle my yard
like majestic gems. They are suddenly surrounded
by killdeer that seem to come from nowhere,
each one seeking the delicate morsels
from the dew moistened earth.
How interesting as each one may look to be the same
yet they are so different. Some more red, others differ
in size and others more aggressive.
Many too busy to be bothered. I am very quiet
as I know that the slightest sound
will send them to flight. Two tiny goldfinches just
flew in seeking their bounty from the earth.
Unlike the robins they depend on the tiny seeds
that fall from the grasses and clover.
As time passes the morning, I will await
another backyard experience.

Spirit Wind

Quivering delight overtakes me
with gay anticipation as
I watch the eagles soar
riding on the winds of time.
It creates an amorous wooing
within the spiritual realm.
Joy comes so easily to my spiritual side,
I sit in awe and passionate delight
as I experience daily, deeper understanding
of my spiritual world.
How delightful the power of the eagle
as it soars above me.
Carrying my Spirit to the wind.

Silent Freedom

Freedom speaks in silence as you
walk the mountains, sit by the creeks
and smile softly at the beautiful meadows.
You can slip into peaceful sleep and
wake to the gentle calling of the birds
as the sun rises slowly in the morning.
The clean clear sound of the creek
can be heard at a distance.
While the water flows you feel
the silence of freedom. As you stretch and yawn,
a deer walks across the meadow.
You breathe the cool crisp mountain air,
and run wild and free like the wolf.
You may even soar among the clouds
on the wings of the eagle as you live and love
in the silence of freedom.

Just for Today

Today is the day to let things happen.
To be an inspiration to yourself, knowing and
accepting the miracles our universe holds for us.
I want to keep my heart and mind open
for the experiences and miracles of my magnificent
surroundings. Focus on gratitude and recognize
the power you have to change your world.
Reconnect yourself to your own creative spirit.
Why be enchanted with just the world around you,
when you have your own treasure chest inside.
Find the exciting things within. When things slow for
me, I know new growth is forthcoming.
I want to understand myself so I can give more freely
to others. I want my own dreams to prosper
so I can encourage the dreams of others.
I gift others by my example. Just for today
I will let things happen.

Through Glass

Looking through a large pane of glass,
I am protected from the elements.
Mesmerized by the splendor before me as
the crisp coolness of fall slips in my world.
The gray autumn sky forms the perfect backdrop
for the deep forest green of the mountains.
The soft, white lacey mist lifts slowly from the valleys
toward the Heavens. A tall, dark magnificent
pine seems etched into the background.
A dry leaf floats ever so slowly toward the ground
and clings to the sumac bush which has now
changed her color to a deep ruby shade of red.
Beneath the etched pine, all the wild grass and brush
have taken on the rustic colors of autumn.
A spot of white from the field of daisies
catches my eye and the beautiful purple thistle
brightens the color of the goldenrod with its richness.
I stand alone in this pristine moment
as a cardinal flies in to add his startling red color
to another precious moment through glass.

Summer Color

At mid-summers song I stop to rest
as the evening sun takes out the palette of paint.
I am in awe of my surroundings
as the sun is slowly setting,
low muted whimsical sounds seem to rise
all around me
as the soft delicate fragrance
of a flowering bush nearby
crosses my senses.
A tender passion for sleep overtakes me.
I lay dreamily across the grass.
Watching as flaming red color
changes the appearance of the water.
The sparkle of a million or more
semi precious stones come to life in front of me
and I awake to a glowing sunlight.

Listening Point

A listening point as the evening glow casts
dark somber shadows across the mountaintop--
knowing the night sounds are not far away.
One by one the sounds come from the dusky shadows,
adding their own special harmony
to this melodious evening.
The sounds encircle me as I try to listen
for one particular note that
may not fit or blend. The soft winds pick up,
adding a little rustling sound
as the leaves touch.
I lie back on the soft earth,
watching the fireflies and seeing
ragged phantom clouds
amble across the dancing moon
from my listening point.

Statue

Lost in the maze of a long weary forgotten garden,
she is exhausted from the long journey.
Too tired to go over the hedge. It was too thick
to crawl through. A tiny form lay crumpled on
the wet grass. The sleep that has eluded her now
takes over and she is lost in the world of "dreams".
She feels something warm as it softly caresses
her body. She sits tall and looks up.
Before her is a statue. It does not move.
She looks at the statue; it talks to her, sees her inner
soul. She feels him run his fingers through her hair.
He wipes the tears from her eyes and holds out his
hand. She places her hand in his; she feels his strength
as he lifts her from the ground. His eyes touch her
with a smile. He fills her with new hope, a new
beginning, and a new life. He may be stilled in stone,
but the passion she feels is like no other. She cannot
take him for her own for he belongs in the garden.
His hand points in a straightforward position. She
takes all he has given her and walks to the direction
he is pointing. She looks back one last time knowing
she could return to her statue in the garden.
THE DREAM

Dancing Clouds

The sky is a beautiful pastel blue
with white billowing clouds
dancing across the mountain tops
like white filmy silk. The faces in the clouds
are too numerous to mention as they
sweep across the heavens to be reborn.
The lightness of the clouds seem to lift and
lighten the tops of the mountains
as they dart up and down in quivering delight,
while riding the wind. They seem to become
entangled in the tops of the tall oak trees
with enthusiasm. The oaks
seem to flaunt their skirts
in acceptance of the joyful
dance of the clouds!

My Warrior

My warrior with eagle wings,
since I met you, many days have passed,
many moons have changed,
and many winds have touched my face.
I have felt the strength of your eagle wings.
The day we met for the first time
still glows like an ember in my mind.
The gentle touch of your spirit
has warmed my inner soul.
My heart is filled with joy and my world
has forever changed since I met you,
my warrior with eagle wings.

The Scrap Quilt

There seem to be a lot of magic colors
in my scrap quilt of life. I have been gathering pieces
all my life and piecing them together one at a time.
If I get a dull color I surround it with others
that are brighter. This helps create a happy look.
Some of the pieces fit right away
and others need to be trimmed.
Some seem a little small
but they are equally important.
I work on this scrap quilt daily and
realize the beauty it holds.
I enjoy the spiritual balance of my life
as the pieces of yesterday
become my colors of tomorrow.
My scrap quilt warms me as
it holds the gentle memories of my life.

My Love

My love for you burst forth
like the most beautiful spring flowers.
The love you return is unmatched,
even by the wildest stallion in all his fury.
You bring into my life the strength of the eagles
as they soar high into the heavens.
The bravery of the most ferocious bear
and the swiftness of the deer.
You give me the peace and beauty of the mist
from the most delicate waterfall.
Our love and your touch
is like no other.

Why Does The Wolf Howl

He feels his inner horizons and answers
the inner promptings of his spirit.
He walks alone on his path,
as do many on the spiritual trail.
At times he is very hungry
and desires food, desires food and water,
but he does not stop. His journey continues,
he listens in great anticipation
to the whispers of the spirits that surround him.
He howls to the moon for guidance.
He does not have to lead the pack but accepts
his own path in life and has faith in his natural world.
He never surrenders to the negative feelings
or despairs. He is strong and active
in the face of threatening odds.
The wolf howls to announce his spiritual presence.

Look For Your Miracles
(It is so easy to feel a miracle)

The tiny bead of water on a lily pad.
The beautiful butterfly in a field of clover.
Seeing a nodding goldenrod on the gentle wind.
The energy of the honeybee as he works.
A grain of sand on the sea shore.
The sparkle of diamonds on a summer pond.
Watching a robin in early spring.
The dance of the clouds in a crystal blue sky.
The smile on the face of a tiny child.
Letting the raindrops touch your skin.
The pungent odor of the moss on the forest floor.
Touching the petal of a delicate rose.
The miniature pebbles at the water's edge.
Deep carved facial lines of the Elders.
The sound of the growing corn.
Admiring the colorful softness of the rainbow.
The dance of the fall winds.
The moon and stars in the evening sky.
Mostly the sound of your inner drum.
LOOK FOR YOUR MIRACLES.
AHO

Still River

Clouds of the heavens and
the surrounding trees seem to be
in an eternal embrace by reflection
as they merge into one in the still river.
I cannot help but wonder
what the still placid water would say
if I ask it to share its memories--
I think it would say, "See the big pine tree
there on your left? I remember his seed
as it fell upon the ground.
That year the winter was harsh,
but the little seed was tucked away
deep inside an old log.
When the spring winds began,
the tiny seed awoke and started to grow.
I shared myself with him and let him drink.
Now he repays me
with his beautiful reflection."
AHO

Sacred Water

Sacred silence, gentle waters have always inspired me.
The waters cleansed me, and inspired my fantasy.
I went to places beyond the sun and to
the core of the earth. Listening, I realize
a more beautiful orchestra will never be heard than
the sounds of water.
From the ocean waves to the falling mist of
the highest waterfall, a more spiritual place
will never be found than at the water's edge.
It has lived in and around all of creation.
A living symbol of life, a sign of humility,
love and joy, our Sacred Water.
Prayers of love.

October 30, 2009

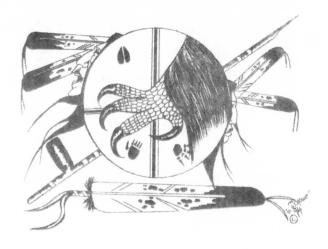

Searching

I watch daily as people search
for what is there, and they never find it.
The ancient teachings are all around us.
Yet many never learn the peaceful, wonderful place
they live in. The world around you is not just
a physical place, it is a mental, emotional, and
spiritual place as well. Let the wonders of
Mother Earth touch you and let the Creator guide you.
Your body is a shrine, a home for your spirit.
Let it be a warm comfortable place.
Again search and fill it with all the
warm treasure and wisdom around you.
Accept what you find, love and feel what you find.
The smallest grain of sand has a story and is filled with
wisdom of another time. Search for your wonders and
make yourself comfortable.

Sea Sand

The sea and the sand, two ancient mysteries
join together in an endless ballet as
the cold fingers of the sea come into the shore
and lie on the breast of the sand.
The trickles of water dance across the sand and slither
slowly back to the sea.
I feel like I am watching a command performance
as it happens before my eyes.
The cool water returns time after time
in perfect harmony and presents a new ballet
in the sand. I have stars in my eyes and
dreams in my heart as I watch
the joining of the sand and the sea.

Kiss Of Life

This morning I felt the kiss of life as it greeted me.
I enjoyed the response to my dreams and needs.
I have the power to receive all of life in abundance.
The dreams of my heart are a part of my special
world. I let the Creator create through me. All of life
is wisdom. I learn from life in all its forms. I extend
my heart and hand as I reach for my wisdom. I am
never alone, I know I am a friend among friends as I
hold myself a lover of life. I want to love without
demanding. My love allows others the freedom of
being themselves. My love is constant and reliable.
My heart explores the world with wonder. My heart
and soul are receptive to the prompting of the spirits.
I enjoy my adventurous journey and I walk it with
courage. I do not let the thoughtless behavior of others
cause me to doubt or forget my own self-worth.
I ask for divine intervention when troublesome events
arise. I know I will receive the help and strength
I need. I am happy today that we share this world
together. My spirit is rich beyond my knowing
as I feel the kiss of life.
AHO

Harp Strings

Quietly I listen to the music of the harp strings,
as they flirtatiously blend with the
music of the water as it rolls over the rocks
and heads for a new adventure in some strange
mysterious place. If only I could be a droplet of water,
creating the wonderful rippling sounds.
I wouldn't mind being the sound leaving the harp
strings. I could certainly relinquish myself
in the beautiful works of art,
being created by such natural sounds.
Here to enjoy for the moment
then lost forever.
A beautiful sound can be heard only once.

My Return

My nude spirit walks sensually
across the garden of time.
How will it be when I
return to the Earth Mother,
exposing my unclad spirit in
pageantry as I travel to another
world, feeling the triumphs of
my past as I try to display
the beauty I found on my path?
Or will my wisdom be null and void,
and teachings from a new
time begin? Something more
complex or intense. How
will it be when I return?

Lost To The Natural World

Looking down from the hillside, I see the
distant ponds. Such sharp delicate lines have
been sculpted by the hands of time. I am alone,
yet surrounded with life. This feeling of oneness and
the timelessness of this vista can only be felt, I think,
when the spirit is at rest. The awareness is so sensitive
that the smallest blade of grass seems to want to say
good morning. The miracle of a tiny stone seems to
call out for recognition, the sound of a tree frog seems
to encompass my inner ear with its melody. The
miniature pink fleecy field flowers beckon my senses
with their delicate aroma. I see the beauty of the tree's
mirrored image in the pond. I walk toward the
shimmering water in hopes of finding an extra miracle
that I had not seen or felt. I was not disappointed.
As the soft gentle fingers of the morning breeze swept
around my face and through my hair, I could feel my
laughter coming from within as my feet slid cautiously,
yet freely into the warm waters of the pond. The
coolness brought a glow to my face as I tenderly touch
the warm placid water with my fingertips…..then
touching my face with the moisture of another time.
The simplicity of this freedom cannot be
described…..it must be felt.
What a blessed and peaceful day.

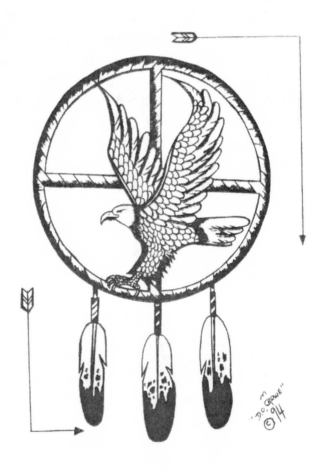

72

Beautiful Dance

Come; stand with me at the Ceremonial Ground.
Listen to the ancient drums and hear the silenced
voices of the singers, as their songs are still heard
in the wind. I look at the Eagle high in the heavens.
He now carries the songs of a new era to the Creator.
With arms uplifted the young warrior steps into
the circle, his eyes find the eagle high above him and
the sound of the drum sets the beat to honor the
Creator. His bare feet sink slowly
into the sand as his painted body starts to
move with the sound of the drum.
The deer toe rattle strapped to his ankles
creates yet another rhythmic sound.
The feathers on his arms seem to come
to life as I watch him dance. I say my
prayers, knowing these beautiful sounds
will carry them to the Creator…
I am enraptured by this beautiful dance.

Stardust

A calm peaceful night on the soft sands
of the beach brings serenity to my soul.
The stars sprinkle the heavens like a sea of diamonds.
What a wonderful night to cry out to my spirit,
and listen in the silence of darkness. I feel lost in the
immensity of the universe. Here is where stardust is
created and dreams come true, as the unspoken lessons
of life come to you. The trees at the waters edge sing
as the night breezes blow their pretty leaves. The
beautiful stars twinkle to the rhythm of the gentle,
mellow wind, as they shimmer together and sprinkle
the night with stardust. The mountain shadows on the
distant shore seem so far away from me, but so close
to the stars that cover them. Somewhere in the silence
I hear the coyote howl.
He must be thanking the stars for their beauty.
The stillness of the night carries the sound of the owl
across the lake. I listen to the stars and ask for wisdom
as the heavens sprinkle me with stardust and
I sleep till dawn.

Clouds to Cloud

Two clouds in the Sunshine of their life,
drifting separated and alone, until the
timeless wind picks up and sails them
together. The current of the wind holds
them. They feel the softness of the
Creator's touch. The clouds now see each
other. They sail slowly, cautiously, and
inevitably on their gentle path. The
winds seem to know what the clouds
have not yet seen, as they both listen
with quiet heart and spirit. The clouds
first touch being gentle and delicate.
With trembling forms they reach out to
each other and enjoy the warming sun
and cooling breeze. They quietly and
tenderly embrace then disappear into
each other, becoming one cloud in
togetherness. They fill the empty spaces
in each other, changing shapes as they
share themselves and enjoy the quiet
drifting as a gentle rainfall from the
clouds…
TEARS OF JOY

Life Is Wonderful

A Golden butterfly etched in black,
stopped by to drink the nectar from my
glass with amorous enthusiasm. Why not taste the
saffron trumpet flowers or the
laughing plum blossoms of white flimsy lace. I am
fascinated as I watch, daring not to move. The desire to
watch this delicate beauty was overwhelming. No
color more perfectly brushed the passion of nature than
the early springtime. Spring itself is eagerness
personified. This time of year is filled with natural
gifts from every direction. Everything around me
seems filled with daring confidence and carried by a
friendly breeze. My golden butterfly just left
flying toward the meadows. In awe I say,
"life is wonderful."

Essence of Roses

As the midnight breeze creeps through the window
beside my bed, I can feel the gentle caresses as
it covers my skin and floats through my hair.
When one tender gust completes its journey,
another is there to replace it with yet another soft
sensual caress. My mind carries me to another time,
a simple life, one without restriction.
Softly the dream waves begin, moving with the wind.
Passionate thoughts of living in the open spaces
invade my mind. The singing silence in the pensive
quiet twilight. The dense green summer foliage of
a sheltered cove and the dew drenched grass
in early dawn. Suddenly I awake to
the essence of roses.

Dew Drops

As I walk across the forest floor,
heavy laden with dew and grasses, I sat against
the giant tree looking upward as the
beautiful golden stands of sunlight filtered
down to the earth's floor to dry up the dew drops,
pulling them upward to moisten the
beautiful plants and trees, creating a misty cloud
on the journey upward, giving them a
new life each day and then waiting for the
evening shades to come so it can
return once again to the forest floor.

Enraptured

Traveling forward, I face a blue gray marbled sky,
with jaded hillsides protruding from the deep
dark silhouettes of the mountains.
I am enthralled with the wonders and
delicate thoughts of you.
I want to stand in the folds of your eagle wings and
feel your breath on my forehead, as I whisper
my haunts and fears of the past,
words that I have never shared with anyone.
I feel that the Creator has blessed me with a
wonderful spirit to nurture me and share my feelings.
I feel blessed with you in my life.

The Wisdom Trail

As I sat across the circle from one of our "old ones",
my mind seemed to leap beyond the tired sculpted lines of
his handsome face. I suddenly saw a baby on a cradleboard
being carried deep into the forest as he gurgled and looked
all around. With the joyful sighs and beautiful bright eyes,
the young one saw everything that moved. The eyes
suddenly closed and a young boy with fawn skin and long
dark hair pranced in front of me. He was shaping a stone
for the stick lying beside him. Soon he would have a nice
war-club to use for play as he joined his friends in the
fields. His features changed before me to those of a young
brave as he drew back arrow after arrow in preparation of a
big hunt that would soon come, as he prepared himself to
be a father, capable of caring for his own family. He now
has a beautiful girl at his side; dressed in white buckskin
she is a sight for any young warrior. He silently slips away
in the night to protect his family. The years pass ever so
quickly as he teaches his children the skills they will need
to carry them along the Good Red Path. He sings quietly to
a soft tiny bundle wrapped in rabbit skin. He knows that
his grandchild will soon fall into his own position and join
the ranks of the Elders, with the same sparkle in his eye and
the same soft sculpted lines of one who has walked the
Wisdom Trail. My thoughts return to the room as I continue
my walk with the "old ones" on the Wisdom Trail.
Aho

Halt Who Goes There?

'Tis the wind who carries the sound.
Our very life sound,
from the past into the future.
The rustle of the leaves.
The swift passing of the fox.
The breaking bark of the bear.
'Tis the wind who carries the sound.
The sound of the baby's cry,
the laughter of a child.
The sigh of a fleeting teen.
The groans of the old.
'Tis the wind who carries the sound.
The smell of the winter smoke.
The spring rain on the window.
The flowers in the summer's meadow.
The shifting of the winter's grain.
'Tis the wind who carries the sound.
From the past into the future.

Beautiful Woman of Time

She glides through the portals of time. Young, sensuous, as
the gauzy print of womanhood has awakened every pore.
She walks and smiles with exuberance,
loving the natural feel of the earth as she crosses the
meadow. Knowing she is a perfect part of a divine whole,
she allows unique souls into her life, being reminded of the
divine spark, she is original, inventive and warm in her
relationships. Each step forward is splashed with the
clinging of fresh silk to the body she so lovingly gives to
time, she chooses every moment a new freshness, for the
heart opens and the love of life enters. The soft breezes
blow across the meadows of time and kiss the moisture
from her face. She breathes with deep affection the delicate
scent of the flowers in the meadow, leaving lasting loving
impressions of time. The aroma clings to her soft supple
breast as she quickly crosses the meadow. Whispers of the
heart are heard here. She allows happiness to shine in
silent chambers. This beautiful woman gathers precious
moments, stores happiness and enjoys sharing her world
with kindness. She is a divine soul, knows she encounters
all she meets with great curiosity and gracious hospitality.
She prepares for yet another time in her life where she will
walk more slowly. Time has aged her beautifully as she
crossed the meadow of life. Embracing all the cooling
breeze, it now leaves the scent of the meadows on her
warm moist body now covered with the gentle lace of time.
A great passion of life has evolved as this beautiful woman
has crossed the meadow of life, felt the arrows of time.
The mind and feelings of the youthful soul
tell their own story.

Remember the Things That Give

Walking the narrow overgrown path around the pond,
I notice in the cattails a delicate and abandoned spider web
as it clings to the decaying seed pods. The little web had
given a home to the spider, a store house for his food. Now
it clings with its last threads to the cattails that once gave it
strength. The natural things around us are always inviting
and interesting. At the edge of the cattails are the remains
of a long forgotten stump, just a little taller than me. The
stump seems to cry out to me, "I am still alive, can you
see?" Yes stump, I can see…I remember your great
outstretched arms, one held my swing…I played many
hours here. I remember when I scraped my feet on your
roots, I was maybe four. I giggled with joy when I
climbed high in your branches. I remember having a picnic
in your shade, yes, that day was fun and I was happy. I
remember sitting with you on days when I was sad…you
felt my warm tears. Your little bugs and insects made me
laugh again. I watched them work and play. I remember
wondering how long their days must be, because they were
so small. I too remember watching the robin in her nest.
How happy she was that you were her home. The squirrels
scampered up and down your trunk and ate your walnuts.
You sure were nice to them too. Yes tree, I hear you and
remember your beauty. Did I forget to say thank you for all
those nice things you did? I appreciate all of them and
honor those memories today. Some times we do forget
what makes our beautiful memories.

Making A Rainbow

I sat with a spool and a lid from a jar.
I added soap and a touch of water. The world
comes to life as I blow bubbles and swirl them
in the air. In the bubbles you can see the ocean blue,
watch the misty valley rise and fall, climb the
mountains and find the entrance to the hidden cave
with excitement. I catch all my bubbles and
put them in a jar. They are beautiful,
light and colorful like the rainbows. I am a being
of love. I want to express myself as I really am.
I listen to the child within myself and set out to
build a rainbow. I have all the colors I need for love
and compassion, the ability to listen to the calls
from within and to see the beauty in others.
I enjoy the spirits of joy and abundance.
I build my special rainbow with all the good things and
invite the butterflies over to inspect the rainbow place.

Let Me Be A Child

Imagination and meditation seem to go hand and hand
with me. In the spring's setting sun, I search for
a special place. Across the lake the waters are silent,
the grasses seem misty from a distance, I see the
sun strands as I walk toward the grass.
I reach a beautiful place; lie on the velvet grass and
feel the warmth. I relax and close my eyes and
my spirit dances in the warm sunshine.
My soul is free and my mind swings in contentment.
The air so fresh, sweet soft breezes ruffle my hair and
carry the perfume of the wildflowers and grasses. I
feel and smell the wonders of life as I meditate. My
imagination carries the eagle on its wind and I watch
the rabbits hop, and the deer jump the fence, the tiny
turtle crawls closer as my spirit dances in the wind, I
am a child again.

Mysteries

The Creator gave us mysteries everywhere you look.
Everything you touch, even your thoughts are
tiny mysteries. Some mysteries can be answered,
some cannot. Some create an expression of awe,
and some just make you giggle, while others become
bigger mysteries. Try writing some of your mysteries
and see how much fun you have.
Why can't I see where my tongue is attached?
Where is the center of the sea and what color is
the scent of the pink roses? Where does the sun sleep
or can I tell the carnation I am thankful for its
fragrance? Which tastes better, the flower of the wheat
or an orchid? Why do the trees lose their leaves in the
cold weather and do the trees really talk?
How can we thank the clouds and where do the waves
go. To whom does the ragged condor report and
how can they fly so far? I was once told there was no
way to answer why. Is this true? I ask myself many
mysterious questions with total innocence and
delight myself with yet another mystery,
WHY

Waiting For New Growth

Gathering the fall flowers in their
colorful dresses, showers me in sweet essence.
Creating thoughts of the beautiful seeds planted and
the tiny shoots that once lifted their tiny arms
to the heavens. Hearing the tiny buds grow,
knowing that soon they would leave
clusters of color everywhere.
They have danced through the season of their life,
leaving their seeds for another time.
They are being cut now to preserve
the beauty of their past and carrying
their aroma to the future.
I too want to leave behind seeds
that will help create new beginnings.

Tears

Do the tears of the ancestors not yet shed
wait in small lakes?
Waiting to be wiped away by our hands?
Can we cherish the companion spirits,
honor them with our talents, abilities
and gifts? They were divinely led and
divinely placed in my path.
They call to the divinity that resides
within each of us. Dignity and kindness
let the love flow to others through
harmony and grace. Do not let the
tears of the ancestors touch the ground.
Turn them into liquid love.
Share them with the world around you.
We are one, let's cherish the unity.

Many Waters

From the mountaintops to the valley below
flow many waters. Stay in tune with the
voices of the past, the calm of today and
the cry of the future.
Today I walk by the peaceful water and
see many faces before me.
Soft gentle hauntings of the past touch
the core of my being. Gentle reminders
to listen, feel and touch the words
spoken without a tongue. Let's sow the seed
and share the stories of the past.
Let them roll across the rapids or
swirl away in the center of a whirlpool.
Gather the footprints along the sandy beach
and catch some of the ancient dreams as
they sail away on tiny leaves. When I walk
by silent waters, I rest, and listen to
the children cry out in peaceful sleep,
wanting to learn. Then comes the roar of the
waterfall heard from far and near. Suddenly a
gentle spring shower brings me back to teach.

Barn Memories

I walked to the old barn hundreds of times,
early dawn and late evenings. My mind
walks today up to the door and smells
the familiar odor of the hay and the animals.
I slide back the latch with one hand and
hold the handle of the gleaming milk pail in
the other. I walk into the barn and hear birds
teetering softly in the rafters and the
scampering of the field mice as the cow bells give
a soft tinkle in the early morning light.
I busy myself dipping the feed and putting it
in the trough for the cow to eat. I pick up the milk
stool, put it in place. A big smile crosses my face as
I realize how deeply this old barn memory
is etched in my mind.

Grandmother's Braids

I remember one cold winter evening when the snow was blowing. My cousins and I walked past the old pine trees and down the path toward our grandmother's house. It was the first snow and the pine needles were not yet covered. We laughed at the blowing snow and screeched at the wind as it passed our cold ears in fury. We passed the old persimmon tree and grabbed a few persimmons from the ground before the snow could cover them. They say persimmons are the best after the first frost so they were great with the first snow.

When we got to the house and started to go inside the wind blew the door open for us. We all ran in and closed the door. Our grandmother began fussing at the stove to heat the milk to make the mush for her girls.

We got out of our wet clothes and laughed as the melting snow dripped from our hair. Soon the sounds of spoons clicking in the cups could be heard as we added honey to our cornmeal drink. Our grandmother set about to warm cloths to dry our hair. She watched our young faces with a smile and giggled because the wet hair tickled our backs and neck. By the time we

finished our warm drink the moon was coming into
view and the dark shadows fell across the room.
The gabby little girls took their place by the fireplace
and waited their turn for grandmother's tender touch.
She dried our hair with a warm cloth, cupped our ears
in her hand and whispered softly to each of us, "Let
your ears hear only the good things in life." We would
all listen to the things she told us. She was indeed our
mentor. After she dried our hair she would make one
single braid in the back, dividing our hair into three
strands. She would sing a little chant, as she would
braid each strand, for each had a meaning. She would
softly say ---

Mind, body and spirit.
Mind, body and spirit.
Mind, body and spirit.

This was said in the most wonderful soothing voice.
Over and over sowing seeds for her granddaughters'
futures. These tiny seeds were planted and we would
long remember her way of combining the mind, body
and spirit together. When she would finish, we were all
ready for the pallets that were side by side on the floor.
This happened of course after each of us got our
beloved treatment and our grandmother's braids.

Beautiful Spirit Lake

I have spent the weekend close to the water
at beautiful Spirit Lake. I love and enjoy the water,
it brings out the best in my thoughts. A purification
of sorts. I feel the soft passionate winds of time as
they skip across the lake. A spiritual uplifting follows,
laced with the aroma of fall. The chill is most
amusing, as it sends my mind to a frozen state.
A journey I want to last, as I watch the geese, herons,
wood ducks, and other water birds prepare for their
migration. Being a bird person this is a unique
paradise. The different species of birds and waterfowl
are great and the numbers are many.
The water is alive with appreciation as I watch
the birds, the gentle winds of time bring me back to
the beautiful sky, which has now turned to more shades
of pink, red, and orange than I can count, as it cast a
radiant image of itself across the beautiful Spirit Lake.
This lake is like a magnet. Drawing not only special
people, but the birds as they travel their migratory
path. What was life like here for my Indian Ancestors,
to have given it this name? They too, must have been
enchanted with the spirit of the water.

Footprints in the Wind

The wind carries the footprints of time.
Where will your footprints go?
Across the mountain so high; to the prairies
below; maybe through marble halls;
a walk on the moon or deep
into the sands of the ocean?
Wherever they go they will weather time
and be blown in the wind.
The prints you leave behind can last forever
or be covered with deeds undone.
I want to leave good footprints to the wind.
Never to be forgotten in the pages of time.
A kindness I may have done for a child
or a smile to a stranger or a talk with a friend.
Where will your footprints go on their timeless
journey in the winds of time?

Rain

To feel the rain is an experience in itself.
Sad that few take the time to enjoy it.
The rain, I feel is like many things, it is a very
personal moment of sharing with nature.
Come walk with me this day. Share the pleasure
as I walk across the grass into the field of weeds.
I want to feel the wonderful feeling
as the weeds welcome me. They bow and
sway in rhythm with the wind. I want them to
touch my skin and share their moisture.
They will never disappoint me as they
dance the elegant dance of the Wind Sounds.
I laugh and twirl in the tall wet weeds feeling
the touch of many. Their beautiful limbs
reach out to stroke me, holding me in a
trancelike state. Their beauty captures my mind
as their moisture caresses my soul.
What a joyous evaluation of such
a spectacular moment.
I always try to leave a part of myself in
appreciation for the beauty that the
Creator has bestowed upon me.
Today the part I would like to leave
are my words as I share them with you.

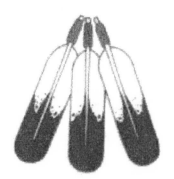